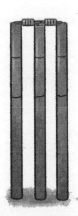

To John, Trevor, Colin and George
and the great times had at OT, Headingley
and Trent Bridge.
C.G.

For all the kids in the world, this is just
a peek at the amazing things you can do.
L.A.

First published in Great Britain 2023 by Red Shed, part of Farshore

An imprint of HarperCollins*Publishers*
1 London Bridge Street, London SE1 9GF
www.farshore.co.uk

HarperCollins*Publishers*
Macken House, 39/40 Mayor Street Upper,
Dublin 1, D01 C9W8

Copyright © HarperCollins*Publishers* Limited 2023

ISBN 978 0 00 860609 1
Printed and bound in the UK using 100% Renewable Electricity at CPI Group (UK) Ltd.
001

A CIP catalogue record for this title is available from the British Library.

MIX
Paper | Supporting
responsible forestry
FSC™ C007454

This book is produced from independently certified FSC™ paper
to ensure responsible forest management.

For more information visit: www.harpercollins.co.uk/green

INCREDIBLE
CRICKET

Written by Clive Gifford
Illustrations by Lu Andrade

RED
SHED

"The best way to be successful
is to be fearless."

– Mithali Raj, Indian batter

Contents

Introduction

Welcome to the wonderful, and sometimes weird, world of cricket. This fascinating and action-packed team sport is played all over the world – from beaches to mountainsides and even once on horseback. Some games are fun hit-abouts between friends, others are epic battles watched by millions between the world's top players vying for a World Cup or Test match glory.

This book is packed with gripping matches, extraordinary players and mind-blowing statistics. From the very chilly game that was played at the South Pole (mind the penguins!) to the team made up of clowns, via epic run chases, the team that scored zero runs and the wicketkeeper who put raw meat in his gloves . . . It's all here!

The language of cricket can often seem complicated. At the end of the book you'll find a glossary with simple explanations of the key terms used in this book. Popping crease? Silly mid-off? We've got you covered!

There is also a section on basic rules of the game and quizzes to test your knowledge. So, wherever you are on your cricket journey, we hope you have fun!

PLAY!

"We should be looking to inspire every living person in this country to play the game of cricket."

– Joe Root

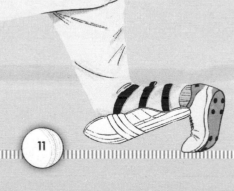

DID YOU KNOW?

If you want to stop a batter from scoring, try bowling a yorker!

The ball pitches near the batter's feet and barely bounces, making it very difficult to hit. Masters of this deadly delivery include India's Jasprit Bumrah, Pakistan's Shaheen Afridi and Australia's Mitchell Starc. England's Jofra Archer has delighted crowds with some explosive yorkers too. The delivery is thought to have been given this name because bowlers from York played it so often!

Playing at the Poles

Cricket has been played in some of the coldest places imaginable . . . including the North and South poles!

Chilly at the crease

In 2005, two frostbitten British explorers trying to walk to the North Pole attempted to play a one versus one game of cricket using an inflatable plastic bat and stumps. Unfortunately, at -45 °C, both the bat and stumps shattered when hit with a real cricket ball. Oops!

Socks on ice

Three years later, Indian and English explorers at the North Pole braved teeth-chattering temperatures of -40 °C to play a match using a plastic spade as a bat and ski poles for stumps. The ball was made of tightly-rolled-up socks! India won the chilly but thrilling five overs-a-side encounter by one run.

Penguin alert!

At the other end of the planet, a one-off game was played at Cape Evans, Antarctica, in 2004. A rucksack was used as the stumps and boat oars as bats. At one point, a giant Arctic skua bird tried

to steal the ball –and later the match had to be abandoned when dozens of Adélie penguins invaded the pitch!

Southern skills

In 1985, a game took place 650km from the South Pole at Bowden Névé. A Hercules transport aircraft had taxied up and down the snow to press it down and turn it into a pitch. The two 14-a-side teams – the Casuals and the Occasionals – were made up of scientists and environmentalists. Roger Wilson of Greenpeace, the environmental charity, top-scored for the Casuals with 22 as they made 102. However, it was the Occasionals who triumphed with a score of 129 – although 13 batters were listed on the scorecard as 'retired, frozen'. Brrrr!

Snowballs

The most southerly cricket match of all occurred in 1969. It featured a handful of hardy players, including New Zealand captain John Reid who used the South Pole marker (a red-and-white striped pole) as the stumps. This meant that every shot he played, no matter which direction he struck it, travelled north!

The game didn't last long. Reid struck a huge six, which landed in a snowdrift and the players' only ball was lost. Game over. In such bitterly cold temperatures, that was just as well!

DID YOU KNOW?

Sir Don Bradman ('The Don') holds the record for the highest number of runs scored during the Ashes: 5,028 runs, between 1928 and 1948.

DID YOU KNOW?

Betty Wilson is one of just six cricketers to have scored over 100 runs and taken ten wickets in a Test match. The second of these all-rounders was Alan Davidson in 1960. Next came England's Enid Bakewell, with the largest run haul of all, a whopping 180, achieved in 1979.

Ian Botham joined them a year later, in 1980, followed by Imran Khan in 1983, playing for Pakistan. Over a decade later, Bangladesh's Shakib Al Hasan became the sixth member of this exclusive club of awesome all-rounders, with a mighty 143 runs and ten wickets!

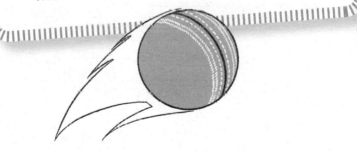

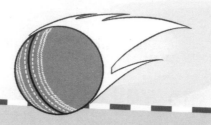

Ellyse's Double Debut

Name: Ellyse Perry

Born: Wahroonga, Australia, 1990

Nickname: Pez, Dags

Country: Australia

Clubs: Birmingham Phoenix, Loughborough Lightning, New South Wales, Sydney Sixers, Victoria

Position: All-rounder (right-hand batter; right-arm, fast-medium bowler)

Famous for: All-round superstar

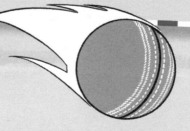

Ellyse Perry had to pinch herself as she stepped out onto the Gardens Oval in Darwin, Australia, in July 2007 . . .

At just 16 years of age, she had been picked to play for Australia versus New Zealand – the youngest Aussie debutant ever. Around her were all the legends of Australian women's cricket, including the best batter in the world, Karen Rolton – one of her childhood heroes. There she was amongst them, wearing the same shirt!

Ellyse tried to quell her nerves as the game, the second ODI of the Rose Bowl Series, got underway. Within a few overs she was called into action. She had been picked as a fast bowler. She came on first change and her youthful pace soon had the New Zealand openers hopping about.

With the score on 41-0, Ellyse beat Maria Fahey's defences to clean bowl her. OUT! She played her second, third and fourth ODIs in the next week – her international career was well underway.

Seven days after playing her fourth ODI, Ellyse found herself walking out into another arena, a hot and humid pitch in Hong Kong . . . a football pitch! She was now playing for the Matildas – Australia's national women's football team. As a sports-mad kid growing up in Wahroonga, Sydney, Ellyse had played almost every sport imaginable – and she excelled at both cricket and football. *This is crazy – two debuts in two weeks*, Ellyse thought.

But she kept her focus. Within two minutes, the ball was at her feet just outside Hong Kong's penalty area. She thought she'd try a looping shot and . . .

GOAL!

The ball crashed into the back of the net. Australia were comfortable 8-1 winners in Hong Kong.

Ellyse was at the start of a very intense five years, trying to juggle playing football and cricket for clubs and her country. One day, she'd be in football training, then media interviews; the next day, it would be a three-hour session in the cricket nets, honing her batting and bowling skills.

In 2012, a year after she had appeared, and scored, at the FIFA World Cup quarter-finals, Ellyse realised she had a choice to make: football or cricket. She knew she couldn't continue to do both at elite level. Ellyse chose cricket and then really began racking up the records . . .

BEST ODI BOWLING 7-22 versus England, 2019

ODI WORLD CUP WINNER (2013, 2022)

11-TIME WOMEN'S NATIONAL CRICKET LEAGUE CHAMPION

FIVE-TIME ICC WOMEN'S T20 WORLD CUP CHAMPION (2010, 2012, 2014, 2018, 2020)

TOP TEST SCORE 213 not out – the highest not out total in women's cricket

THREE-TIME ICC WOMEN'S WORLD CRICKETER OF THE YEAR (2017, 2019, 2020)

In 2020, Ellyse was voted ICC (International Cricket Council) Female Cricketer of the Decade. From fast bowler, she's become the world's best all-rounder, lethal with bat and ball, and a global cricket superstar. When not playing for Australia, she's wowing fans in the Women's Big Bash and starring in leagues in India and England.

"You've always got to be evolving," she says, "I always want to try and get a bit better and do things a little differently."

So what advice does she have for young cricketers, starting their own journey?

"Go for it, give it your absolute best shot. Listen to people but hold on to your own confidence and self-belief, it's your greatest tool for success."

DID YOU KNOW?

Blind cricket star Steffan Nero has also represented Australia in goalball, football and futsal.

Prickly Wicket

A hedgehog managed to stop play in a 1957 Gloucester versus Derbyshire County Championship match. The prickly customer refused to move from the wicket, so wicketkeeper George Dawkes made good use of his thick gloves to carry it away to safety.

DID YOU KNOW?

When making his ODI debut in 1996, Pakistan all-rounder Shahid Afridi used a bat previously owned by Indian cricket legend Sachin Tendulkar. It must have suited him as he hit the world's fastest ODI century at the time, in just 37 balls!

Feel the Buzz

A 2019 World Cup game between Sri Lanka and South Africa was stopped by bees. As the bees swarmed around the pitch, the players and umpires dropped to the floor to avoid being stung! Bee-have!

Strangely, the same two teams faced a similar incident two years earlier at the Wanderers cricket ground in South Africa.

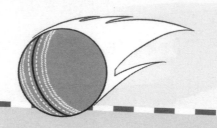

Oh, Jimmy, Jimmy!

Name: James Anderson

Born: Burnley, England, 1982

Nickname: Jimmy

Country: England

Clubs: Auckland, Lancashire

Position: Bowler (right-arm, fast-medium)

Famous for: Outstandingly accurate swing bowling

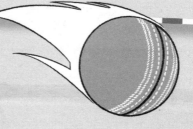

Fast bowling is really hard work. You have to sprint in, leap and hurl your body forward, whirling your arm over as fast as possible to bowl the ball quickly and on target. Then you have to trudge all the way back to the top of your run-up and do it all over again. James Anderson, known to his fans as Jimmy, has done this more than 37,900 times for England in Test matches alone.

Then, there have been 9,584 balls bowled by Jimmy in ODIs and thousands and thousands more for his first club, Burnley, then his county side, Lancashire. In 2022, he turned 40 years old. When Jimmy first played for Burnley Cricket Club in 1998, his England teammate Ollie Pope was just four months old, while Sam Curran and Harry Brook hadn't even been born!

Jimmy made his England debut in ODIs in 2002 and in Tests the following year. He has played in Test matches every year since, 177 of them so far, taking 675 wickets – the most of any fast bowler.

What's more, he shows no signs of retiring. In fact, his bowling figures have got better the older he gets. In 2021, he recorded his best ever bowling figures for Lancashire – 7 for 19 – and in 2022, he took 36 Test match wickets, at an average of 19.8 runs – outstanding!

Whilst England fans chant "Oh Jimmy, Jimmy! Jimmy, Jimmy, Jimmy, Jimmy Anderson!" every time he bowls the ball, opponents are in awe of his skill and fitness. As for Jimmy himself, he reckons:

"As long as I am fit, contributing to the team and bowling well, then who knows how long I can go on for? Maybe 50 is a stretch but we will see!"

– Jimmy Anderson

Good Luck, Bad Luck

Cricketers can be a superstitious lot. Here are just a few of the strangest beliefs and rituals dreamt up by players and followers . . .

No-go numbers

In Australia, the number 87 is thought of as bad luck: an unlucky 13 short of a hundred. In England, the number 111, known as Nelson, is considered bad luck. So is double Nelson (222) and triple Nelson (333).

No one is certain where the superstition comes from, but it is common in local cricket in England, possibly because 111 looks like three stumps without the bails on top! The name Nelson may possibly come from a New Zealand team called Nelson. They played their first first-class cricket match in 1874 and scored 111. The team finished playing in 1891, when their last ever innings score was – you've guessed it – 111 again. Freaky!

Famous umpire David Shepherd used to be seen hopping from foot to foot when a team's score reached 111, 222 or 333. "When I was kid playing village cricket down in Devon," he explained.

"We found the only way to counteract something bad happening on a Nelson number was to get your feet off the ground . . . If I was on the field of play I would jump or hop."

Individual players have superstitions too – even tough cookies like former Australian captain Steve Waugh. He always batted with the same red handkerchief in his pocket, given to him by his grandparents. Shubham Gill also carries a red hankie for luck, whilst West Indian all-rounder Andre Russell always taps his bat four times on the ground before facing every ball.

A kiss for luck

Sri Lankan bowler Lasith Malinga used to kiss the ball every time he ran in to bowl. Bearing in mind he

bowled more than 18,000 balls for Sri Lanka
and over 20,000 more for club teams, that's
a lot of kisses!

Wash it lucky

Australia's Meg Lanning likes to sit in the corner of
a dressing room before a game – a seat anywhere
else will not do. Meg's teammate Jess Jonassen
washes all the clothes she wears when she plays well
and her team wins, so she can wear the exact same
outfit in the next match.

Getting it right . . . or left?

Even the great Ellyse Perry has a superstition, always
putting her right sock, shoe and pads on first. Indian
legend Rahul Dravid also insisted on putting on his
right pad first, whilst his teammate Sachin Tendulkar
plumped for the left pad first every time.

Ceiling the deal

South African batter Neil McKenzie would avoid treading on any of the white lines marking out a pitch during a game – hard when you're bowling or trying to make a run! He also made sure that all the toilet seats were down in the changing rooms before he went out to bat. For a while he would even tape his cricket bat to the dressing-room ceiling until he needed to go out and bat with it!

DID YOU KNOW?

Legendary wicketkeeper-batter MS Dhoni famously wore the number 7 jersey, which he picked because he was born on 7th July – and NOT because he considers the number 7 to be lucky!

Bella the Elephant

Cricket has its ducks and rabbits (tailend batters that cannot bat well) but, in 1971, it had an elephant too.

Yes, really!

Bella was borrowed from Chessington Zoo for India's Test match versus England at the Oval, in London. She arrived at the ground and was paraded around the outfield to give the Indian team good luck.

It worked! India recorded their first ever series victory in England by winning this match. Thanks, Bella!

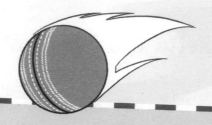

Brian's Big Score

Name: Brian Lara

Born: Santa Cruz, Trinidad and Tobago, 1969

Nickname: The Prince

Country: West Indies

Clubs: ICC World XI, Marylebone Cricket Club, Mumbai Champs, Northern Transvaal, Southern Rocks, Trinidad and Tobago, Warwickshire

Position: Middle order batter (left-hand)

Famous for: Legendary batting and record-breaking innings

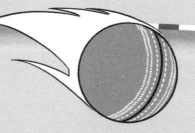

West Indian batting genius Brian Lara played youth football and table tennis for Trinidad and Tobago before he decided to focus on cricket. With his high backlift, grace and effortless striking, he was soon scoring LOTS of runs for Trinidad and Tobago, then the West Indies.

A shaky start

The year 1994 was a big one for Brian. He set a world record score of 375 in Test matches (he would later score an even bigger Test knock of 400).

In the English County Championship, Brian had already scored five centuries for Warwickshire by the time his team faced Durham. Brian started badly. Durham bowler, and Brian's West Indies teammate, Anderson Cummins, nearly got him out first ball. Brian had inched his way to 18 runs when

Simon Brown's delivery caught the edge of his bat and the ball sailed towards the wicketkeeper's gloves. Chris Scott was an experienced keeper and said, "It was a catch I'd taken a million times before . . . very straightforward . . . regulation." He dropped it and held his head in his hands. "He'll probably get a hundred now," people in the crowd muttered.

They were right. Brian ended the day on 111 not out.

Blistering form

The next day's play saw Brian score another 174 runs before lunch – an incredible feat. As the game went into its final session, the crowd started realising that something special was happening. The record for highest-ever score in a first-class match, 499, had been set by Hanif Mohammad in Pakistan in 1959 and few had ever got near it. But Brian had got to 400 and he was still going strong . . .

Failing to score

After passing 450, Brian was tiring and the overs left were running out. He entered the last over on 497, just three runs short of setting a new world record. He couldn't score off the first ball or the second, or the third.

The fourth ball was a surprise bouncer which hit him on the helmet. Brian had just two shots at glory left . . .

Record runs!

It turned out he only needed one. Brian cracked the ball to the boundary, his 62nd four of his innings. The crowd went wild. Brian had scored 390 runs in a single day to reach 501 not out – an incredible record that still stands. "I never actually looked at 50 or 100s as milestones," he reflected later.

"Rather, I fell in love with batting long."

And he really did: Brian's career contained 34 Test hundreds, 19 ODI and 65 first-class hundreds.

DID YOU KNOW?

Brian is one of only two cricketers ever to score two quadruple centuries in first-class cricket. The other player to achieve this extraordinary feat is Aussie legend Don Bradman.

No-ball Haul

A six is also known as a 'maximum' as it is usually the most runs a player can score from one ball – although there are exceptions. If a bowler bowls a no-ball, for instance, one or two runs are added to the score, plus any the batter scores and the ball has to be bowled again.

During a 2016 match in Australia's Big Bash League, Travis Birt of the Hobart Hurricanes hit a six off a no-ball bowled by Clint McKay. When McKay bowled again, the same thing happened – another no-ball and Birt hit another six. Oops! Next time, McKay managed to bowl a fair delivery, but again Birt struck a six, meaning he had scored 20 (6+6+6+2 for the no-balls) off one delivery. Amazeballs!

What's in Your Gloves?

Cricketers are always on the lookout for clever ways to improve their game and get the edge over the competition. Sometimes their solutions can be downright bizarre . . .

In the case of Australia's explosive batter Adam 'Gilly' Gilchrist, the answer to the question 'What's in your gloves?' was . . . a squash ball. Yes, really! Gilchrist placed the ball inside his bottom hand glove on the advice of his batting coach, Bob Meuleman, to help with his grip.

It certainly paid off! In the 2007 World Cup final versus Sri Lanka, Gilly smashed his way to a match-winning 149 runs off just 104 balls, with the squash ball providing hidden help.

England wicketkeeping legend Alan Knott opted for something more meaty to protect his hands when fielding and taking balls from fast bowlers. Knott was known to place raw steaks inside his gloves to cushion the blows. Imagine the stink at the end of a long, hot day in the field!

DID YOU KNOW?

The first World Cup in cricket was for women and won by England? Find out more on page 58.

Wilson's Wickets

In 1958, Australia's Betty Wilson became the first player, male or female, to take 10 wickets and score 100 or more runs in the same Test match. In 29 overs bowled across the two innings against England, she took 11 wickets for just 19 runs. Her performance included the first ever hat-trick (three wickets taken in three balls in a row) in women's Tests. Epic!

DID YOU KNOW?

Betty Wilson is one of just six cricketers to have scored over 100 runs and taken ten wickets in a Test match. The second of these all-rounders was Alan Davidson in 1960. Next came England's Enid Bakewell, with the largest run haul of all, a whopping 180, achieved in 1979.

Ian Botham joined them a year later, in 1980, followed by Imran Khan in 1983, playing for Pakistan. Over a decade later, Bangladesh's Shakib Al Hasan became the sixth member of this exclusive club of awesome all-rounders, with a mighty 143 runs and ten wickets!

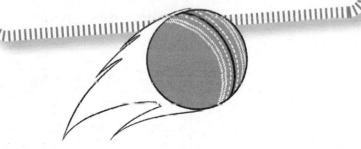

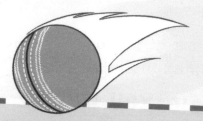

World Cup Wonder

Name: Anya Shrubsole

Born: Bath, England, 1991

Nickname: Hoof

Country: England

Clubs: Berkshire, Perth Scorchers, Somerset, Southern Brave, Southern Vipers, Western Storm

Position: Bowler (right-hand, medium-seam)

Famous for: Bowling fast and taking vital wickets, often with lethal inswingers

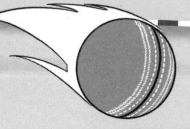

The 2017 Women's ODI World Cup pitched England against India in front of a sold-out crowd at the home of cricket – the Lords ground in London.

India had restricted England to 228 and were cruising into the 180s with plenty of overs left and seven wickets remaining. England captain Heather Knight turned to her faithful fast bowler, Anya Shrubsole, for her final spell. Anya had bowled one of India's opening batters for a duck in her very first over several hours earlier, but knew if she didn't strike quickly, India would triumph.

Anya's first two balls were thumped to the boundary by India's in-form batter Veda Krishnamurthy, but later in the over, she trapped Punam Raut LBW (leg before wicket). Anya turned and roared her appeal to the umpire and was relieved to see his finger go up.

Anya's teammate Alex Hartley took a wicket in the next over but it was Anya's next over where the fireworks flew.

Changing her pace and angles, she tricked Veda Krishnamurthy into a poor shot which was caught, then speared a fast ball through Goswami's defences to rattle the stumps. India were now 201-7 and the tension was mounting.

Anya, though, remained calm and focused. She knew what she had to do. A run out occurred before another wicket fell to her devastating bowling. India's last pair needed 10 runs. It seemed as if it was all over as Anya forced the last Indian batter to loop the ball up into the air . . . But – noooo! – Jenny Gunn dropped an easy catch. Whilst her teammates looked dismayed, Anya gestured for them to re-focus:

"Don't worry, I've got this. It will happen."

And happen it did, the very next ball, when an awesome delivery struck Rajeshwari Gayakwad's off stump. Out! Anya screamed with delight as she was mobbed by her teammates.

India were all out for 219. They had lost their last 7 wickets for 28 runs, five of them to England's star fast bowler. Anya's final figures of 6-46 were the best of any bowler at a Women's World Cup final and the best by any England ODI player at Lords, male or female.

"I was first here watching my dad play in the club national knockouts," recalled Anya, whose father is former county cricketer Ian Shrubsole. "So to be back 16 years later as a World Cup winner is just amazing."

Tidal Test

If you've ever complained about a cricket pitch being a bit damp, think again.

The Bramble Bank is a 180m-long sandbar between Hampshire and the Isle of Wight. It only rises above the water for a short time when the tide goes out. A game of cricket was played on the sandbar in 1954. One team was led by a famous sailor called Uffa Fox. The other was a team of inmates from Parkhurst prison, on the Isle of Wight. Fox's team won by seven runs, but they were using rowboat oars as bats.

Today, the tradition of playing matches on Bramble Bank is going still strong. Members of two rival boat clubs, the Island Sailing Club and Royal Southern

Yacht Club, race to the sandbar as it emerges from the water. Their mission: to play a once-a-year game of quick cricket – there's less than 90 minutes before the sandbar is submerged. The players play in full cricket whites with the only change in kit being wellies or bare feet.

In 2018, the Royal Southern boosted their team with England legend, Stuart Broad joining in the fun. According to John Allen, the opposing skipper:

"He hit one ball of mine so hard it was more like a 12 than a six. It just disappeared into the distance and someone had to go out and swim to retrieve it!"

A Smashing Six

Taxi driver Asif Ali's delight turned to horror as he hit a huge six in a 2021 Halifax Cricket League Cup quarter final match: he watched it sail over the boundary only to smash the rear windscreen . . .

. . . of his own car!

As Ali sank to his knees, his opponents from Sowerby St Peter's, and even the umpires, began to laugh. Ali said later:

"The shot felt great coming off my bat, I knew it was going to be a big one. After that, it was really hard to focus on the game."

Ali went on to make a creditable 43 runs but his side lost the match by seven wickets. Meanwhile a video of his smashing six went viral!

Squid Game

South African Daryll Cullinan hit a truly sizzling six during a 1995 Castle Cup match between Boland and Border in South Africa. The ball sailed high over the boundary and straight into a red-hot barbecue on which a fan was grilling calamari (squid).

The game was delayed by ten minutes whilst the umpires waited for the ball to cool down so they could clean the grease, ash – and squid – off it!

Did the hungry spectators finish their seafood meal after the ball landed in the BBQ? No one knows. But the ball did end up being replaced: even after being thoroughly cleaned, it still was too greasy for the bowler, Roger Telemachus, to handle!

Giddy Up!

A 1794 cricket match took place in Linstead Park, Kent, between the Gentlemen of the Hill and the Gentlemen of the Dale . . . all on horseback. Bowlers galloped in to bowl and batters tried to hit the ball using specially-made bats with very long handles. Sadly, the scorecard from the game has been lost, but it remains a great tail. Er, we mean *tale*!

DID YOU KNOW?

Around 500 years ago, the game of 'stoolball' was played by milkmaids, using a turnip as a ball and milking stools as a bat or wicket. Stoolball is thought by some historians to be the forerunner of cricket!

Pioneer Against Prejudice

Sometime in the 1950s, a policeman came to break up a game of kids' cricket that was blocking a road in Wolverhampton. He took down the names of all the players except one – because she was a girl and in his words:

"Girls don't play cricket."

The girl, whose name was Rachael Heyhoe Flint, was furious. She loved cricket! She was just as furious when she played with her older brother and he made her field all day in the flower beds, no matter how many times she got him out. When she finally got the chance to bat, he wasn't able to bowl her out for three days! As he stormed off to play football with his mates instead, Rachael practised alone by dangling a ball on a string from a roof gutter. She spent hours

striking the ball until her arms ached and
the gutter fell off!

Rachael was 16 when she played her first women's
county cricket game, taking six wickets with her spin
bowling. She first played
for England in 1960,
and six years later
was made captain.

In Tests, Rachel averaged
45.5 runs every time
she went out to bat.
In ODIs, her average was even higher, an amazing
58.5 runs. In her 12-year spell as skipper, England
never lost a Test series. Incredible!

It turns out girls *do* play cricket!

Rachael would spend much of her life fighting prejudice in order to get more chances for women to play cricket. She battled cricket clubs that only admitted male members, fought for resources to establish girls' cricket in schools, and campaigned for money and publicity to encourage women to play cricket and to send women's teams on overseas tours. Appalled at the lack of coverage of women's matches, she turned her hand to journalism, and began sending in reports to the newspapers herself. Her energy seemed limitless.

The first World Cup

Rachael was also a keen football fan and supporter of Wolverhampton Wanderers, better known as Wolves. She got to know a fellow Wolves supporter and businessman called Jack Hayward and, in 1971, the pair came up with a plan to hold the first ever cricket World Cup. The tournament was held in 1973 at grounds all over England and featured Australia, New Zealand and Jamaica amongst the seven sides, each playing all the others in games of 60-overs-a-side games. The players were women. Rachael ended up scoring 257 runs during the tournament and lifting the trophy at Birmingham's Edgbaston cricket ground.

Since 2020, English women's teams have competed in the annual Rachael Heyhoe Flint Trophy competition. In international cricket, the world's best female cricketer receives the Rachael Heyhoe Flint award each year.

DID YOU KNOW?

Rachael's legacy is commemorated by the Heyhoe Flint Gate at Lord's Cricket Ground.

Steve's Shed

Did you know that Joe Root, Steve Smith and Virat Kohli's thigh pads and arm guards are made in a small garden shed in Australia?

The story began in 1985 with a cricket enthusiast called Steve Remfry, who made splints at Adelaide Children's Hospital. Whilst watching a game on TV, he saw how Indian batting legend Sunil Gavaskar was struggling with a flimsy forearm guard against Australia's fierce fast bowlers. Arm guards and similar body padding were new at the time. In fact, some cricketers stuffed a thin paperback book into their trouser pocket to act as a thigh guard.

Remfry knew he could do better . . .

Perfect protection

He fashioned a stronger foam armguard at work and dropped it off at the Adelaide Cricket Ground for Sunil. It must have suited the batter as he made 166 not out! Word spread and soon top cricketers, from Kapil Dev to Shane Warne, flocked to Adelaide for Steve's made-to-measure protective clothing.

A family business

Now in high demand, Remfry started making the gear in a small shed in his back garden, equipped with a grinder, sewing machine and a pair of hair straighteners to seal the stitching on the straps. Steve's son, Luke, now makes Remfry thigh guards and other protective equipment in a similar way in his own garden shed.

Ducks That Were Quackers!

A duck is when a batter is out without scoring. It got its name because a zero looks a bit like a duck's egg on the scorer's chart. As a cricketer, it's the last thing you want as you head out to bat!

So what about a golden duck? Spoiler: it's worse! This is when you are out without scoring on the first ball you face. Don't fret if it ever happens to you, though. ODI World Cup winners MS Dhoni, Jason Roy and Suresh Raina all suffered golden ducks in their first ODI games for their country.

A diamond duck is when you are out without scoring OR even facing a ball. Usually, this means you've come in to bat but are at the non-strikers end and are run out before you even get to play a shot.

But, believe it or not, there's even worse . . .

A king pair (of ducks) is the fate dreaded by all batters. It's when you get a duck in both innings of a match. It's pretty rare in Test matches. When Jimmy Anderson suffered one in 2016, it was the first by an England cricketer in 110 years. Ouch!

In 1999, New Zealand's Geoff Allott bagged the opposite of a golden duck. Well, sort of . . .

Whilst playing South Africa, he blocked and blocked and blocked for 141 minutes and 77 balls but was *still* out for a duck, the longest in Test match history!

In 1913, two Somerset clubs contested a game. Glastonbury's players were down after only scoring 80. They needn't have worried. Here's the scorecard of their opponent, Langport:

C.J. Manley	lbw b Lisk	0
F. J. Pittard	b Lisk	0
J. Lang lbw	b Lisk	0
A. Knight	c Lukins b Lisk	0
W.E. Brister	b Baily	0
H.E. Cozens	b Lisk	0
H.G. Stigings	lbw b Lisk	0
H.B. Hamm	b Baily	0
L. Parker	b Baily	0
H. Weaver	not out	0
F. Barningham	b Lisk	0
TOTAL		**0**

The Don's Duck

The most tragic duck of all occurred back in 1948 at the Oval in front of a sell-out crowd. England were facing Australia's all-conquering team, nicknamed the Invincibles because they didn't lose a single one of their 34 tour matches. England were bowled out for just 52 but many in the packed crowd didn't mind. It meant they got to see and cheer on the world's greatest batter as he played his very last innings.

More than average

Sir Donald Bradman, aka The Don, was a cricket legend, still considered by many as the best batter in history. Best of all was his batting average – the number of runs scored divided by the number of times out. Bradman's average as he strode to the wicket against England at the Oval was 101.39.

Extraordinary! Batting superstars today like Joe Root and Virat Kohli have averages of around 50 – half of the Don's.

Back at the Oval, all eyes were on Bradman as he faced spinner Eric Hollies and defended his first ball. The second, though, fizzed through his guard and, to the surprise of the crowd, thumped into the stumps. The Don was gone . . . out for a duck. The crowd were in shocked silence. If Bradman had scored just four runs, he would have ended his illustrious career with a batting average of precisely 100.00. His duck meant he finished with 99.94. So close!

As he trudged back to the dressing room and sat down beside teammate Neil Harvey, all the world's greatest batter said was:

"Fancy doing a thing like that."

THE DON: CAREER STATS

211 CENTURIES

50,731 RUNS

THE ONLY PLAYER TO SCORE 12 DOUBLE CENTURIES (200 runs or more) **IN TEST CRICKET**

SCORED THE MOST TEST RUNS IN A SINGLE DAY: 309 in 1930 versus England.

THE ONLY PLAYER EVER TO SCORE CENTURIES IN SIX TEST MATCHES IN A ROW, ALL AGAINST ENGLAND

DID YOU KNOW?

You can be out leg before wicket (LBW) with ANY body part in front of the stumps – not just your leg!

Sachin Tendulkar was out LBW with his shoulder when he ducked into a ball bowled by Australia's Glenn McGrath in a 1999 Test match! Tendulkar scored zero runs that day, but he went on to score 15,921 Test runs during his career – the most of any player EVER.

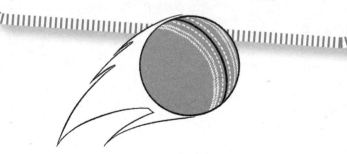

Teen Talents

Cricket has always attracted talented youngsters. In July 2014, Gaby Lewis made her debut for Ireland in a women's ODI against South Africa. She was just 13 years, 166 days old. By the time she left her teens, Gaby was a cricket veteran, Ireland's all-time leading run scorer and the first Irish woman to score a century in a T20 game – thumping 105 runs off just 60 balls including three sixes. In 2022, at the age of 21, she also became her country's youngest ever captain.

Amazingly, Gaby isn't the youngest ever international cricketer. When the Ireland team played a series of ODIs against Pakistan in 2000, they faced 12-year-old Sajjida Shah. Sajjida became famous for her off break bowling and appeared in 60 ODIs and eight T20 internationals.

Sajjida was the 2003 IWCC Trophy tournament's leading wicket-taker. She had destroyed the Japanese team, taking seven wickets for just four runs. Outstanding! These remain the best bowling figures in the history of women's ODI cricket – and an amazing performance from Sajjida, who was just 15 at the time.

More Tremendous Teens

With only 120 balls for a team to score off, notching up a T20 hundred is a tough task . . . The youngest player to do so in an international game was Gustav McKeon in 2022. The 18 year old smoked 109 off just 61 balls for France, playing against Switzerland. Amazingly, it was only Gustav's second international match. Bien joué, Gustav!

Freya Kemp made her county debut for Sussex in 2019 having just celebrated her fourteenth birthday. The exciting all-rounder has since played in the Hundred, the Rachael Heyhoe Flint Trophy, T20 international games for England and appeared at the 2022 Commonwealth Games . . . all before her eighteenth birthday!

It's Raining Sixes

Before he became a one-day star for Lancashire and England, Liam Livingstone played club cricket for Nantwich. In 2015, his side faced Caldy Cricket Club in a 45 over-a-side competition. Liam was nearly bowled on the third ball he faced. *The wicket's slow,* he thought. *I need to hit some sixes here.*

He did — and some! In the next 135 balls, Liam hit 27 sixes and 34 fours, scoring an incredible 350. Nantwich ended up on 579-7. In reply, Caldy could only make 79-9, losing by a staggering 500 runs. Liam's flurry of sixes saw more than a dozen balls getting lost in the neighbouring cemetery!

Mountain Madness

Cricket is always played on a cricket field, isn't it? Think again . . .

In 2014, a group of 25 cricketers from around the world, including England spinner Ashley Giles, South African fast bowler Makhaya Ntini and England women's captain Heather Knight spent seven days trekking up the slopes of Mount Kilimanjaro In Tanzania, Africa's highest mountain – and a dormant volcano!

Cricket in the crater

Once they reached the volcano crater, 5,752m above sea level, the two teams, Gorillas and Rhinos, rolled out a long cricket mat and planned to play a full T20 game under normal ICC rules. However, the conditions were anything but normal! There was ice and craggy rock, and clouds descended into the crater. The players battled altitude sickness and temperatures as low as −20 ºC. They ended up playing only 10 overs a side because low clouds inside the crater stopped them seeing clearly!

Mt Kili Madness

The match, known as 'Mt Kili Madness' holds the record for the highest game of cricket ever played. Heather Knight, who captained the Gorillas, came away victorious, top-scoring with 21 and taking a wicket as the Gorillas beat the Rhinos by 14 runs.

At this altitude (about four and a half times higher than the peak of Ben Nevis in Scotland), the air becomes really thin, making the ball fly fast off the bat – and 10 sixes were struck!

"This is absolutely incredible! We are playing cricket on the summit of Africa!"

– Ashley Giles

Rock Bottom

Mountaintops aren't the only unusual place where cricket has been played. In December 2013, two English teams, Threlkeld and Caldbeck, both from Cumbria, descended 600m below ground into Honister Slate Mine in the Lake District, the last working slate mine in England.

The teams couldn't play on the rock-hard mine floor so they rolled out a long strip of matting to act as the wicket whilst the umpire placed pieces of slate on top of the stumps for bails! The umpire and players all wore caving helmets for protection. Caldbeck won the game with 10 balls to spare, and the whole match helped raise money for their opponents, Threlkeld, whose ground had suffered flood damage.

Air Miles

Some pro cricketers are real globetrotters, but few can compete with Pakistan's Abdur Rehman. He played in a 2012 ODI against Australia in the United Arab Emirates that finished early in the morning, took a flight to England and bowled for his county side, Somerset, later that day. No jet lag for Abdur, as he took three wickets in that game!

DID YOU KNOW?

England batter-wicketkeeper Alec Stewart's date of birth was 8/4/63. He ended up scoring 8,463 Test runs!

Nero the Hero

In 1922, two blind factory workers in Melbourne, Australia, created a whole new form of cricket.

Instead of a standard ball, they used a tin can containing some small rocks. Using this innovation, the batter could hear the can rattling as it was bowled underarm . . .

Blind cricket was born!

Six years later, the first official match was held between the Australian states of Victoria and New South Wales. The can was replaced by a large plastic ball containing ball bearings or bells, but bowling underarm remains.

In blind cricket, teams are made up of a mixture of completely and partially blind players. The stumps, made of metal tubes, are larger than in regular cricket and umpires shout out their decisions rather than just making hand signals. Other than that, most of the other rules are the same – and so is the thrill of the game!

The bowler calls "play" when releasing the ball and the ball must bounce twice before it reaches the batter. Batters listen carefully for the ball approaching and usually strike it with a sweep shot.

At the very first Blind Cricket World Cup in 1998, Pakistan's Masood Jan scored 262 versus South Africa. This record innings was only beaten in 2022 when Australia's Steffan Nero plundered 309 in only 140 balls versus New Zealand at the International

Cricket Inclusion Series. Steffan's triple century came a few days after he had scored 113 and 101 not out in T20 matches, also against New Zealand. Talk about Nero the Hero!

"It's a dream in itself to play
for Australia so to make
a century for Australia is one
of those lifelong memories you
will never forget."

– Steffan Nero

DID YOU KNOW?

C.B. Fry played 26 Tests for England, appeared in football's FA Cup final for Southampton and, in 1093, equalled the world long jump record of 7.18m. What an athlete!

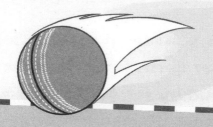

Short Cut to Success

Name: Shafali Verma

Born: Rohtak, India, 2004

Nickname: Shafali

Country: India

Clubs: Birmingham Phoenix, Haryana, Sydney Sixers, Velocity

Position: Opening batter (right-hand)

Famous for: Demon batter and the youngest player to represent India in a T20

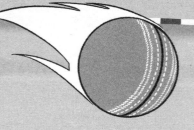

It was 2013 and the stands of the Chaudhary Bansi Lal Stadium near Rohtak, India, were packed with excited fans watching the great Sachin Tendulkar as he played his last domestic cricket match, a Ranji Trophy game. Among them was nine-year-old Shafali Verma, perched on the shoulders of her father, Sanjeev, as she cheered Sachin on.

Shafali came from a cricket-mad family and she would often play in the street with her friends. Her dad could see she was talented, but when he took her to local clubs in the hope she could join a team and play proper matches, they were afraid of letting a girl join in.

However, Shafali wouldn't take no for an answer and she had an idea: *What if I cut my hair? I don't think anyone would notice I'm a girl.* Her father wasn't sure, but Shafali insisted. She got a really short haircut and, amazingly, her plan worked!

Training hard and absorbing knowledge from her coaches, Shafali made an instant impact in her first full season playing for Haryana, scoring 1,923 runs, including three fifties and six hundreds. A run machine!

In 2019, aged 15, Shafali became the youngest Indian T20 player . Two months later, she scored her first international 50, notching 73 runs off 49 balls against the West Indies. This made her the youngest ever Indian to score an international half-century, ten months younger than the previous record holder . . . her idol, Sachin Tendulkar!

Spider or Six?

At some modern stadiums, Spidercams (Flying Fox Cams in Australia) run along cables high above the pitch. They give amazing aerial views of the match – and there's a little-known cricket law about them. If the ball hits a Spidercam, then it's a 'dead ball', meaning batters cannot score runs off it.

Fast-scoring Australian Glenn Maxwell was playing for Australia in a 2018 T20 match versus India. He slogged the ball high and with power, and expected to see the umpire raise his hands to signal six runs – enough to take Glenn to his half-century. But as the ball soared away, it struck the Spidercam and fell to the ground. It was a dead ball, no runs were added, and Glenn was out three balls later. Unlucky!

Nicholas Makes a Promise

Name: Nicholas Pooran

Born: Couva, Trinidad and Tobago, 1995

Nickname: Pooran

Country: West Indies

Clubs: Barbados Tridents, City Kaitak, Guyana Amazon Warriors, Islamabad United, Kerala Kings, Khulna Titans, Kings XI Punjab, Melbourne Stars, Multan Sultans, Mumbai Indians, Northern Warriors, St Kitts and Nevis Patriots, Sunrisers Hyderabad, Sydney Sixers, Trinbago Knight Riders, Trinidad and Tobago, Yorkshire

Position: Wicketkeeper batter (left-hand)

Famous for: Skilful, quick run scoring

The teenaged Nicholas Pooran was hot property. The young batter started playing for Trinidad and Tobago's Under-19 team when he was only 14 and was later picked for the West Indies Under-19 World Cup team. Amongst his match-winning innings at the tournament was a cracking 143 versus Australia – the highest individual score against the fearsome Aussies at U-19 level.

Things were looking very promising for Nicholas, until he was involved in a terrible car crash while driving back from training. When he woke up the next day he was in hospital, both his legs in plaster casts. Nicholas had smashed his left knee and right ankle. After surgery, he couldn't move his knee joint at all. His doctors feared he might never walk again.

Nicholas's recovery was slow. For most of the first six

months of rehab, he was confined to a wheelchair. But he kept faith with the physiotherapists and other medical staff. The desire to play cricket burned fiercer than even before. He made a promise to his family and his girlfriend, Alyssa, that not only would he return to cricket, he would be playing for the West Indies by the time he reached 21.

Gradually, with patience and hard work, Nicholas's legs got stronger and movement returned. He returned to cricket in 2016 and in September was picked to play for the West Indies against Pakistan in a T20 international. He was, you've guessed it . . . 21!

Nicholas's old fluency with the bat returned and he was playing the game with even more passion than before. For a while, he stuck to T20 matches as he feared longer versions of the game might put too much stress on his injured legs. But then he got a call up for the West Indies 2019 World Cup team.

Although his side did not do well in the competition, Nicholas scored more runs than any of his teammates, including 63 against England and a great century (118 in total) versus Sri Lanka.

Then came the highlight of his career so far. In May 2022, just under a year after he and Alyssa were married, Nicholas was made the captain of West Indies ODI and T20 teams, following in the footsteps of his West Indies cricket heroes – and setting himself up to inspire generations of future players!

"Sometimes I'd taken cricket for granted, but now I want to enjoy every single game – I've learned that you never know what's going to happen."

– Nicholas Pooran

Helmet History

The cricket box – a protective cup worn down the front of men's trousers – has been used to protect private parts since its invention in 1874. Amazingly, though, it wasn't until the 1970s, 100 years later, that people started to give thought to protecting their heads from fast-flying balls. Until then, players batted bare-headed or wearing a sunhat or cloth cricket cap. Um, dangerous!

English batter Patsy Hendren was the exception. In the 1930s, he wore a strange-looking cap, made by his wife, Minnie, which contained strips of rubber padding for protection. Good thinking, Patsy.

Thinking a-head

In 1977, English batter Dennis Amiss was about to join

a limited overs competition in Australia called World Series Cricket. One of the teams he would be facing regularly in the competition was the West Indies.

The West Indies team was packed with devastating fast bowlers, including Michael Holding, Wayne Daniel and Joel Garner. There would also be the Australian XI (eleven-player team), featuring tearaways like Dennis Lillee and Jeff Thomson, the sort of super-fast bowlers that gave batters nightmares. There had been some serious cricket injuries already that year, so Dennis decided to do some preparation before travelling to Australia. He visited a Birmingham company called Vellvic, to see if they could help . . .

Hello, helmets!

When Dennis strode out to bat later that year, he wore a motorcycle helmet with a clear, shatterproof visor in front of his eyes and nose. The crowd booed him and shouted, "Where's yer motorbike?"

Some of the crowd may have scoffed, but other cricketers saw sense. Those in charge of World Series Cricket ordered a batch of helmets from Vellvic and, within a few years, many top batters chose to wear helmets when facing pace bowling. Phew!

DID YOU KNOW?

West Indies legend Sir Vivian Richards was the hardest-hitting batter of his day. He struck 35 centuries and 90 half-centuries in Tests and ODIs. In 1987, he became the first player to score a century and take five wickets in an ODI match – a feat not equalled for 18 years!

Losing It

When you next lose a match with your team, don't
fret. Here's why . . .

Lots of cricket teams do poorly, but few do worse than
Dera Ismail Khan, Pakistan. Their first ever first-class
match was against Pakistan Railways in 1964.
In the first innings, Pakistan Railways notched up
a cool 910-6 declared. Wow!

Dera Ismail Khan managed just 32 in their reply and
five less in their second innings to lose by an innings
and 851 runs. The team didn't play again for 20
years. When they returned to first-class cricket briefly
in the 1980s, they lost nine and drew one of their
ten matches!

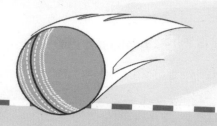

Amazing Chandra

Name: Bhagwath Subramanya (BS) Chandrasekhar

Born: Mysuru, India, 1945

Nickname: Chandra

Country: India

Clubs: Karnataka

Position: Bowler (right-arm)

Famous for: Devastating leg spin bowling

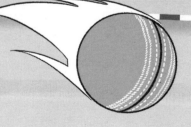

Born in Mysuru in 1945, BS Chandrasekhar, known as Chandra, suffered a bout of polio when he was five. He lost feeling in his right hand and the muscles in his hand, wrist and arm wasted away. Chandra spent much of his childhood playing badminton and table tennis left-handed but also began working tirelessly on bowling cricket balls with his weakened arm.

Gradually, some strength and feeling returned to his hand. Chandra was clever too: to make up for a lack of power in his right arm, he ran in like a medium pace bowler but actually bowled leg spin. He also fielded and threw the ball back with his left arm.

At just 18 years old, Chandra was chosen to play for India. He would play 58 Test matches as a right-armed leg spin bowler, taking an astonishing 242 Test wickets, including 12 in a single match versus Australia in 1978. Few batters could deal with his surprising pace and spin. Legendary West Indian batsman Sir Viv Richards called him "the most teasing bowler I ever had to face. I never quite knew whether I was in charge or not. That was his greatness . . . He could do things with the ball that seemed supernatural."

DID YOU KNOW?

Cricket looked very different in the distant past. Teams of two, three or four might contest matches, with a ball bowled underarm and a bat looking like a big, curved hockey stick. Over time, the rules and equipment evolved to the game you see today.

Toe-tal Legend

Hard-hitting New Zealand batter Martin Guptill lost three of his toes on his left foot in a forklift accident aged just 13. Footwork and balance is a key part of being a successful batter, but with hard work and creativity, Martin overcame this setback to pursue his passion for cricket as a professional.

He has scored over 7,300 ODI runs, including securing the ODI World Cup's record highest score of 237 not out against the West Indies in 2015. Martin's outrageous innings contained 11 sixes and 24 fours.

During the opening match of the T20 World Cup in 2019, Martin injured one of his two left toes – and played the rest of the tournament on just one good toe!

The Timeless Test

Buckle up! One 1939 Test match took 12 days and there still wasn't a winner!

It occurred in Durban, South Africa. England were the opponents and it was the fifth and last Test before they were due to sail home. The rules at the time were that the game had to be played to a finish, however many days it took.

With two rest days, interruptions for rain and a lot of slow play, the game plodded on. England missed their boat back home but figured out they could take a train to catch their ship in Cape Town at the end of the twelfth day.

With five wickets left and needing just 42 more runs, England had a sniff of victory – before more rain fell at tea and snuffed out any chance of an exciting ending. So, after 5,447 balls bowled and 1,981 runs scored, the game was declared a draw. Phew!

DID YOU KNOW?

Australian captain Pat Cummins has been ranked the world's number one pace bowler – not bad for a player who lost the top 1cm of the middle finger of his bowling hand. The cause? His sister slammed the door on his fingers when he was four years old. OUCH!

One-match Wonder

Australian Roy Lindsay Park was a real all-rounder. Turning 21 in 1913, he juggled studying to be a doctor with a passion for sport, particularly Aussie Rules football and cricket.

On the cricket pitch, it wasn't long before Roy's skilful, patient batting began attracting attention, and he was called up to the Australian cricket team for their 1914-15 tour of South Africa. But World War I broke out and the tour was called off. Instead, Roy completed his medical training and joined the Australian Army Medical Corps. Off he went to Europe by ship to tend the wounded in battle. He didn't return to Australia until 1919, a year after the end of the war.

The following year, aged 28, Roy finally got his chance to shine, against Australia's fiercest enemy, England, at MCG (Melbourne Cricket Ground). Roy had spent the night before delivering a baby and he had barely got any sleep, but still he felt confident. After all, the last game he'd played at the MCG had seen him score a faultless 111.

The score was 116-1 as Roy strode out to bat. He had waited six years to prove himself. His wife, Alice, was watching in the stands, her knitting needles in her hands – she was knitting in between balls and overs.

English fast bowler, Harry Howell raced in and bowled. In the stands, Alice dropped her wool and bent down to retrieve it. The ball crashed into Roy's stumps.

OUT!

As Alice retrieved her wool and looked up, she saw her husband trudging back to the pavilion, out first ball. She had missed his innings!

Roy was determined to take his second chance in the next innings. But Australia piled on the runs, scoring 499, then bowled England out cheaply and asked them to bat again. Roy bowled one over during the match which went for nine runs and no wickets.

Roy was never picked to play for Australia again – that pesky ball of wool had caused Alice to miss her husband's entire Test batting career! But happily Roy wasn't the last Test cricketer in the family . . . In 1942, Alice and Roy's daughter, Lal, married Ian Johnson, who played 45 Test matches for Australia, 17 of them as captain of the side.

DID YOU KNOW?

Roy is not alone. In the men's game, there are over 430 'one-Test wonders', and counting!

Amongst them are Trinidadian Andy Ganteaume, who played for the West Indies in 1948, and achieved one of the highest Test batting averages of all time. New Zealand opener Rodney Redmond scored a century in his only Test in 1973 – but despite this was never selected again.

The women's game also has its share of one-Test wonders, among them England's Sonia Odedra and Fran Wilson.

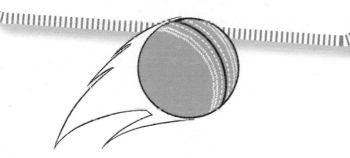

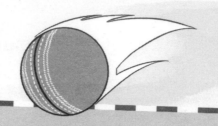

The Ball of the Century

Name: Shane Warne

Born: Upper Ferntree Gully, Australia, 1969

Nickname: Warnie

Country: Australia

Clubs: Hampshire, Melbourne Stars, Rajasthan Royals, Victoria

Position: Bowler (right-arm)

Famous for: Reinventing leg spin bowling

Fast bowling dominated Test cricket in the 1980s and early 1990s. Spin barely got a look in until the arrival of a blond Australian called Shane Warne. Shane was a leg spinner. This very tricky form of spin bowling was thought of as old-fashioned in the modern game. But Shane was determined to prove everyone wrong.

The unknown Aussie

When Shane arrived in England for the 1993 Ashes series, he was an unknown. At the time, there weren't all the video clips and analysis of new players like there are today, so the England team, captained by Graham Gooch, knew little about him, his style and strengths.

The game was on. England were comfortable at 80-1 when Australian captain Allan Border signalled for Shane to bowl his first over. Gooch's batting partner, Mike Gatting, was to face Shane's first ball. Gatting was England's best player of spin and had just clubbed a meaty boundary to get his eye in. He viewed the blond youngster, his face smeared with sun cream, confidently. What was there to fear?

At the other end, Shane felt dazzled by the moment: "Woah! I'm actually bowling my first ball in an Ashes series." He decided to spin his first delivery as hard as he could. He trotted in a couple of paces and, with a fierce twist of his wrist, sent the ball fizzing through the air, crackling with spin.

What happened next stunned everyone.

The ball drifted and dipped away from Gatting before landing 30cm outside leg stump. It then turned violently, ripping past Gatting's bat and hitting his off stump. The bails tumbled and the Australian fans screamed with delight. Shane was as surprised as anyone! Even the umpire, Dickie Bird, was impressed. He turned to the young bowler and said, "Shane, you will put yourself into the record books." He was right. Warne went on to take eight wickets in the match and 34 in the Ashes series. He quickly became one of the world's greatest spin bowlers, feared by batters for his skill, flair and tactical brain as well as his mastery of different deliveries like the Zooter, the Wrong 'Un and the Flipper. The exciting way Shane played inspired young players from Rashid Khan to Alana King and Sophie Ecclestone.

Thirteen years later, Shane produced another piece of leg spin magic to bowl Andrew Strauss, in an Ashes Test in Melbourne. It was Warne's 700th Test wicket – the first player to ever reach that milestone.

"That ball changed my life on and off the pitch."

– Shane Warne

Ben vs Baz

Only three batters have ever hit more than 100 sixes in Test cricket: the Aussie great Adam Gilchrist, England captain Ben Stokes and the current coach of the England cricket team, Brendon 'Baz' McCullum. Ben and Baz are so competitive that instead of normal training before a 2022 Test match in Pakistan, they roped other England players into a six-hitting competition. Coach Baz won!

At the start of 2023, Ben and Baz are tied on 107 sixes each. Ben could console himself with knowing that he was bound to hit a six in future – and with Baz retired from playing professionally, he is bound to become the leading six-hitter. Not that he cares much about personal glory. When it comes to cricket, Ben is all about putting the team first!

From Ball Game to Ballroom

Fancy footwork in cricket can be useful in other competitions. Two *Strictly Come Dancing* champions were former Test cricketers, Darren Gough and Mark Ramprakash, whilst a third, Chris Hollins, has played first-class cricket for Oxford University.

DID YOU KNOW?

Mark Ramprakash scored 1,000 runs in a single season a whopping 20 times. He exceeded 2,000 runs in a season three times.

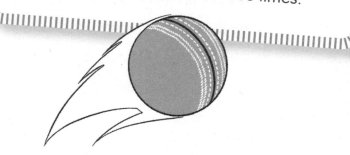

Clowning Around

In 1870, a Cambridge University team won a cricket match against a team of 14 circus clowns. The clowns, whose names included Jolly Seal, toured all over the country playing matches, usually losing but providing plenty of entertainment!

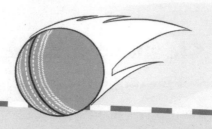

Snowball Strikes

Name: Elizabeth Snowball

Born: Lancashire, England, 1908

Nickname: Betty

Country: England

Clubs: Hampshire, Lancashire, The Rest, West Women, Women's Cricket Association

Position: Wicketkeeper-batter (right-hand)

Famous for: Helping win the first ever women's Test match in 1934

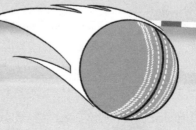

Betty Snowball was only 1.52m tall but her brilliant eye and sharp reflexes helped her become the best female wicketkeeper in the world.

As a child, Betty was a natural at sports. She played lacrosse and squash for Scotland, then, encouraged by her cricket-mad father, Thomas, took up cricket, becoming a batter and wicketkeeper.

After school, Betty went to St Andrews University and then Bedford Physical Training College to train as a teacher. She also got some valuable cricket coaching from the great West Indian cricketer Sir Learie Constantine. He said that Betty hit the ball harder than most men.

In 1934, an invitation came from Australia, asking for an England women's team to travel and compete against them. Betty was delighted to be selected, even though the tour lasted six months and actually *cost* her money. Instead of being paid like today's cricket superstars, all the players had to pay £80 – well over £4,000 in today's money – just to go on the trip. Betty and her family rustled up the cash and they waved her off from Tilbury Docks in October 1934.

The players kept themselves active during their 32-day voyage on the SS *Cathay* liner by playing cricket on deck. They had to be careful not to hit the balls overboard! After arriving in Australia, Betty was proud to open the batting for England in the first ever women's

Test match. In front of thousands of spectators in Brisbane, she ran out the dangerous Ruby Monaghan and ended up scoring the winning runs as England comfortably beat Australia.

Stumped!

For their second Test, the teams moved on to Sydney: the scene of Betty's first record feat. 'Stumpings' are where a wicketkeeper gets a batter out by gathering the ball and hitting the stumps whilst the batter is out of their crease. They're a real test of a wicketkeeper's speed and technique, and are quite rare. Jos Buttler was a wicketkeeper in 35 Test matches for England and only managed one stumping. Betty notched four in a single innings. It's still a joint world record in women's cricket, almost 90 years later!

England won two and drew one of the three-match

series – but there was little time to celebrate. The team hopped on another ship, this time sailing to New Zealand for the second leg of their tour. Betty was still in fine form, scoring 103 and 108 in warm-up games, so was really looking forward to playing against New Zealand at Lancaster Park in the city of Christchurch.

Test thrashing

Betty's teammate Myrtle Maclagan was a demon bowler and opening batter. She had taken 20 Australian wickets in the three Tests and took a further five here as New Zealand were all out for just 44 in their first innings. Maclagan joined Betty at the crease for the start of England's innings but was out early. Betty saw partners come and go as she stuck to her task. Some of New Zealand's bowling was short and wide and she used the square cut – one of her favourite shots – to accumulate a lot of runs.

Betty struck 23 fours before she was caught by Marge Bishop off the bowling of Ruth Symons. Her score of 189 in England's total of 503 made sure England won the match. It was a score that would not be passed in women's Test cricket for 51 years – and is still the highest score made by a women's Test wicketkeeper. Betty nearly added a second century later on during that tour – she was on 99 but was suddenly run out. Agonising!

England's women's team didn't play another Test match for 11 years. When they did, against Australia, Betty was still amazingly in the side, although, now aged 40, she couldn't repeat her run-scoring feats. She later re-trained as an umpire and umpired a women's Ashes Test match in 1951. She retired from playing cricket but continued to teach it, and maths, to schoolchildren in Herefordshire.

Hurray For Hockley

Debbie Hockley is not as famous as she should be. A right-handed batter and right-arm medium bowler, she is considered to be one of New Zealand's greatest female cricketers.

This cricketing legend was the first woman to play 100 ODIs (she totalled 118) and the first to reach 4,000 ODI runs. She was also the first to play 40 or more matches in ODI World Cups, winning New Zealand's one World Cup trophy as part of the triumphant 2000 team. She averaged over 51 runs each time she batted in a World Cup game. After her long playing career, she notched another first, becoming the first female President of New Zealand Cricket in 2016. Legend!

DID YOU KNOW?

The youngest ever player, male or female, to score a double century in ODI cricket, was 17-year-old New Zealander Amelia Kerr. Her whopping 232 against Ireland was the third-highest individual score, male or female, in an ODI – and the highest ever Women's ODI score.

Amelia also took five wickets for 17 runs in the same match. Wow!

Wheely Good

In the UK, wheelchair cricket is an exciting six-a-side parasport played indoors in a sports hall. The hall is divided up into zones worth one to six runs depending on where the batter strikes the ball. A shot straight down the ground is the most likely way to score a four. The bat has a short handle and is

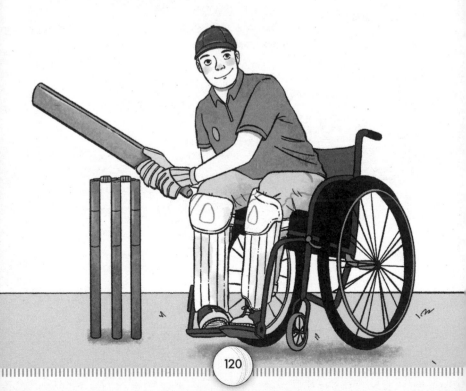

lightweight enough to be used either one- or two-handed. Matches are typically 12 overs per team.

In Bangladesh, India, Nepal and Pakistan, 11-a-side wheelchair cricket teams play on outdoor cricket grounds, drawing large crowds. The Indian Wheelchair Premier League (IWPL) is a yearly tournament, founded in 2018. Teams include the Kolkata Knight Fighters and Chennai Superstars, coached by Vikas Lamba. Batters regularly strike sixes whilst fielders need great wheelwork to chase and recover the ball.

"We are not bound by our disabilities. Rather, they give us the push we need."
– Vikas Lamba

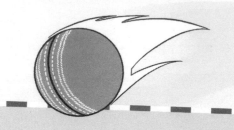

The Accidental Cricketer

Name: Mignon du Preez

Born: Pretoria, South Africa, 1989

Nickname: Minx

Country: South Africa

Clubs: Hobart Hurricanes, Manchester Originals, Melbourne Stars, Northerns, Sussex, Trent Rockets, Warriors

Position: Top order batter (right-hand)

Famous for: Inspirational batting

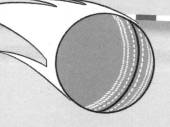

Mignon du Preez's first game of cricket was by accident. Aged just four, she used to go along and support her brother's Under-7s team in Pretoria, South Africa, where her dad was the team's coach.

All kitted out

Mignon was always dressed in the team's kit – it was what she loved to wear the most. When her brother's side was a player short one day, Mignon stepped in, encouraged by her dad. It was a tournament match – and she won the Best Batter of the Day award!

Having played cricket with boys' teams at primary school, Mignon moved to on to high school and starred for the girls' team. Aged 12, she got her next lucky break: a place on the the provincial squad. "Someone had pulled out," Mignon explained later. "I was informed only the night before the game that

I'd have to help out the Gauteng Northern Girls Under-13s team. That was a special day for me." The game was 40 overs-a-side and Mignon thrashed the opposition, scoring a mind-blowing 258 runs, which included 28 fours and a staggering 16 sixes. That's the same number of sixes Joe Root hit in 32 T20 international matches for England!

Legend in the making

Chance came calling again when Mignon was 17. She had trained with the South African national team, the Proteas, but had never been selected. Shortly before an upcoming tour to Pakistan, Shandre Fritz got injured and Mignon got another last-minute invite, while standing outside school.

Mignon secured her place on the squad. She went on to play more than 200 times for South Africa, scoring more than 5,500 runs in ODI and T20 games, and in 2019, her name was immortalised on one of the entrances to the SuperSport Park stadium in Gauteng.

"In your career you might actually have more failed attempts than successes and you need coaches, friends and family around you that will encourage you to keep going when you feel like giving up."
– Mignon du Preez

DID YOU KNOW?

Cricket balls have been made from the same materials since the 1700s – cork, rubber and twine on the inside, leather on the outside. Red balls are used in most cricket whilst white balls were introduced when ODIs started being played as day-night games, as they are more visible. Pink balls have also been used for Test matches played under floodlights.

Dream Debut

When Rehan Ahmed made his debut for England against Pakistan in Karachi in 2022, he became England cricket's youngest male Test player. He was just 18 years, 126 days old.

Ahmed was born in Nottingham on August 13, 2004, the day before Jimmy Anderson took his first Test wicket on his home ground of Old Trafford, versus West Indies. Yes, Jimmy was playing for England before Rehan was born!

Rehan's debut went well. His tricky leg spin bowling took two wickets in the first innings and five wickets for 48 runs in the second. He became the youngest debutant of any nation to take a five-wicket haul in an innings. Amazing!

Short 'n' Tall

There's only ever been one Test cricketer who's been seven foot tall.

Mohammad Irfan played for Pakistan in the 2010s and stood 2.16m (7ft 1in) tall – the tallest ever Test player.

At the other end of the scale stands Kruger van Wyk. The New Zealand batter-wicketkeeper stood 1.5m tall. He played nine Test matches. Although their playing careers overlapped, the pair never faced each other in Test matches.

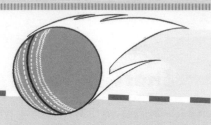

Ticket to Success!

Name: Mahendra Singh (MS) Dhoni

Born: Ranchi, India, 1981

Nickname: Mahi

Country: India

Clubs: Air India Blue, Asia XI, Bihar, Bradman XI, Chennai Super Kings, East Zone, Help For Heroes XI, India Board President's XI, International XI, Jharkhand, Rajasthan Cricket Association President's XI, Rest of India, Rising Pune Supergiants, Sehwag XI

Position: Batter-wicketkeeper (right-hand)

Famous for: Legendary batter-wicketkeeper and ice-cool finisher of ODI games

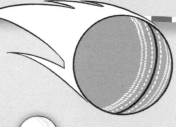

Mahendra Singh Dhoni is one of the legends of Indian and international cricket. He was the first Indian batter to strike 200 ODI sixes. He captained Chennai Super Kings to IPL (Indian Premier League) glory on four occasions, and led India to number one in the Test rankings. Now retired from cricket, he is a multi-millionaire and co-owns several hockey and football clubs.

But life didn't always go his way . . .

As a youngster, Mahendra wasn't certain he could make a career in cricket. In his teens he played for Bihar in the Ranji Trophy, but failed again and again to be selected for India's Under-19s squad. Eventually, he moved away from his home town, and his team, to work for Indian Railways as a ticket collector.

But MS didn't give up on cricket. He trained and played whenever he could, carefully honing his skills – he would even write notes on his thigh pads before going out to bat!

His hard work paid off. Finally, aged 23, MS was picked to play for India in an ODI against Bangladesh. But it didn't go as planned . . . He didn't take a catch or stumping as wicketkeeper and when it was his turn to bat, was run out first ball. Disaster!

Staying the course

There was no way MS was giving up now though. Absolutely no way! He bounced back, a few matches later, to score a rousing innings of 148 – the highest score made by an Indian wicketkeeper.

MS was rocketing to success. He went on to captain

his team in Tests, ODIs and T20 matches a record 332 times. No one has led their country's cricket team out more often. These appearances included the 2011 ICC World Cup, where MS hit a soaring six from the last ball to win the final tournament in front of 42,000 home fans.

Bat's a wrap

Three months later, MS held a charity dinner to raise money for orphans and abandoned children. He auctioned the bat that won the World Cup and it went for £100,000, making it the most expensive piece of willow ever!

"A loss makes you humble. It tests the other batsmen and bowlers. Also, if you keep winning you don't know what area you need to work on."
– MS Dhoni

Dropped by Dad

Andrew 'Freddie' Flintoff was the Ben Stokes of the 2000s, an impressive all-rounder whose skills included taking sharp and spectacular catches as a fielder. His Dad, Colin, who played club cricket, also claimed to be a great fielder. This was put to the test in 2004 when Freddie was playing for England against the West Indies at Edgbaston.

Colin was watching in the top tier of the Ryder Stand when his son launched an ENORMOUS six. The ball sailed high over the boundary. Of all the 20,000 spectators it could have reached, it flew straight towards Freddie's father. "I should have caught it," Colin said later. "I saw it coming all the way but it bounced out of my hand." Oops!

Freddie spotted the fumble from the pitch and thought it was hilarious:

"He got all excited and he put it down, didn't he? I'll have a go at him later!"

Freddie went on to make his highest score in Test cricket that day, a swashbuckling 167.

DID YOU KNOW?

Unlike in most sports, the shape of a cricket ground isn't fixed. It can be circular or oval and varies in size too. However, the pitch, in the centre of the ground, IS a fixed size for competitive games, measuring 20.12m (66ft) long and 3.05m (10ft) wide. It's carefully looked after – a grass pitch will be mown very short.

Awesome Ashes

The smallest, yet most famous, trophy in international cricket is a tiny 10.5cm-tall pottery urn. It's fought for by England and Australia in the Ashes series. So how did this unusual trophy come into being?

Well, it all started as a joke . . .

In 1882, England were heavily defeated by Australia at the Oval in London. Disappointed by the outcome, the English newspaper *The Sporting Times* published a mock obituary:

'In Affectionate Remembrance of English Cricket'.
It joked that 'the body will be cremated and the ashes
taken to Australia'.

Australian cricket fans thought this was hilarious,
and when England travelled to Australia a few weeks
later, they presented England captain Ivo Bligh with
a little urn of ashes as a joke. Ha! It stood on Ivo's
mantelpiece for 44 years, and is now on display at the
Marylebone Cricket Club (MCC) Museum at Lords.

No one knows the origin of the ashes inside the urn.
Some believe they are the remains of a burnt bail that
sat on top of the stumps or the remains of the leather
covering of a cricket ball. It's a mystery!

The Ashes teams now battle for a glass replica of
the famous urn.

Bell-ebration!

Doesn't it feel great to know that your family are proud of your achievements? Cricketers are no different . . .

Sir Curtly Ambrose was a fearsome West Indian fast bowler of the 1980s and 1990s. Whenever he took a wicket in Test matches, his mother, Hillie, ran out of her house in the tiny Antiguan village of Swetes and rang a bell in the street.

She must have had a sore arm as Curtly took 405 Test wickets in total, including seven wickets versus Australia for just one run. Ding-ding!

"If you're good enough, you don't need to say anything to win."

– Curtly Ambrose

Perfect Ten

In 2021, Ajaz Patel became the first New Zealander (and only the third player ever after Jim Laker and Anil Kumble) to take all 10 wickets in a single innings of a Test match. What's more, it was an away match against India's mighty batting line-up. Unfortunately, Ajaz's celebrations were cut short when his team were 62 all out, 263 runs behind India's total. He was the not-out batter at the inning's end. Better luck next time, Ajaz!

DID YOU KNOW?

At 5 foot 6, Ajaz Patel had doubts about making it in first-class cricket as a fast bowler. So, he decided to turn to spin bowling – and the rest is history!

Commanding Kohli

Virat Kohli is India's most successful captain, winning 40 Tests between 2014 and 2022. An absolute run machine, Virat has scored 27 Test centuries, 44 ODI (one-day international) centuries and is the fastest player to have reached 12,000 ODI runs.

If that wasn't enough, Virat is also an Indian Premier League (IPL) legend, playing for Royal Challengers Bangalore. No one has scored more runs than Virat in the world's premier T20 (Twenty20) club competition: 6,624 before the 2023 IPL season including five centuries.

> **"I love playing under pressure.
> In fact, if there's no pressure,
> then I'm not in the perfect zone."**
> – Virat Kohli

Making a Stand

In a 2006 Test versus South Africa, Sri Lanka were in a spot of trouble. Their score had gone from 4 for 1 to 14 for 2 in just the fourth over when captain Mahela Jayawardene came out to join the silky smooth Kumar Sangakkara at the crease.

South Africa were licking their lips at attacking the pair but didn't take a wicket for another 157 overs! During that time, Kumar and Mahela notched up a HUGE partnership of 624 runs. Mahela top-scored with 374. Kumar 'only' scored 287! It's still a world record and no Test batters since have got within 150 runs of it.

"The 624-run stand against South Africa, I don't know but somehow we managed to bat together for nearly two-and-a-half days. It was a very special partnership."
– Kumar Sangakkara

These two extraordinary cricketers began their international partnership when they were both in their twenties (they were born just a few months apart). But they had known each other for much longer . . . Kumar and Mahela had been playing together since they were 15, competing in school cricket matches.

The pair have scored almost 6,000 runs together in ODIs and even more in Tests. They also scored 822 runs in partnership in T20 internationals between 2000 and 2015.

> "We needed each other out there in the middle . . . It was good to have a friend, someone I could share the good and bad times with."
> – Mahela Jayawardene

Twelfth Man

What happens when a player gets injured mid-game – or needs a change of bat or gloves? It's time for the 'twelfth man' to step up!

This is the name for the reserve player (or, more likely, players – there is usually more than one) who wait patiently on the boundary edge, offering support to the team. Their duties have changed over the years –

DID YOU KNOW?

The world's biggest cricket bat was 32m long, 4m wide and weighed 950kg – about the weight of 12 Ben Stokes!

It was displayed outside the ICC Academy in Dubai, in the United Arab Emirates, in 2015.

these used to include serving drinks to the team and even making lunch!

Many Indian cricket fans will be familiar with Dharamveer Pal, the unofficial twelfth man of the national team, who accompanies them to almost all their matches. Dharamveer suffered from polio as a child and was captain of the disabled cricket team of his home town, Madhya Pradesh, until moving to Delhi. As unofficial twelfth man, he has spent time with star players including Virat Kohli, MS Dhoni and Yuvraj Singh – plus international legends like Shane Warne and Chris Gayle!

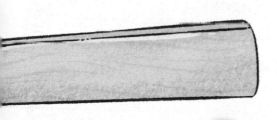

Super Scorer

Who scored the fastest century in ODI history?
AB de Villiers, that's who!

AB scored a century in just 31 balls against the
West Indies in 2017. The South African batting
maestro only failed to score off four of the 44 balls
he faced in total. He blasted nine fours and an
incredible 16 sixes in his incredible final score of 149.
AB's score chart read:

421146466 ○ 2211666461411 ○ 44 ○ 64666166646622 ○ **Out!**

"I really hate it when I can't score runs from a ball."

– AB de Villiers

Extra Slip?

The first recorded cricket match on ice was played in 1766. Chesterfield played Sheffield on the frozen reservoir waters of a dam near Brampton, Cumbria. Despite all the slipping and sliding about, Sheffield scored 125 runs and won.

DID YOU KNOW?

Pakistan fast bowler Shoaib Akhtar, nicknamed 'The Rawalpindi Express', bowled the fastest known ball in cricket history at the 2003 World Cup. His dynamite delivery was clocked at 161.3 km/h – that's RAPID!

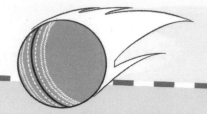

Big Ben

Name: Ben Stokes

Born: Christchurch, New Zealand, 1991

Nickname: Mr Incredible, Stokesy, The Dragon

Country: England

Clubs: Canterbury, Durham, Melbourne Renegades, Northern Superchargers, Rajasthan Royals, Rising Pune Supergiant

Position: All-rounder (left-hand batter; left-hand, fast-medium bowler)

Famous for: Game-changing performances with the bat, ball and fielding – as well as being a truly inspirational and innovative captain

Ever since he burst onto the world stage as a fiery all-rounder in the early 2010s, Ben Stokes has been box office, taking bursts of vital wickets, scoring big runs and making some of the most spectacular catches ever seen on a cricket pitch.

"No way, no, no way, you cannot do that, Ben Stokes. That is remarkable, that is one of the greatest catches of all time!"
– Nasser Hussain, Sky commentator
and former England captain.

In April 2022, England announced Ben Stokes as the country's 81st permanent Test captain. The Test team had suffered a rough couple of years, only winning one Test out of 17 matches. By the time Ben tucked into his Christmas dinner that year, the side had won nine out of ten Tests under his command. What a turnaround!

> **"We're trying to rewrite how Test cricket is being played."**
>
> – Ben Stokes

What's the secret? To make Test cricket as fast, fun and entertaining as possible. He instructed bowlers to focus only on taking their opponents' wickets. Don't worry if they score lots of runs off your bowling! Batters were told to go out there and enjoy the occasion, score fast, show off all their shots and attack the opponents' bowling. If you get out, well, it happens. Don't worry about it. Ben, and England coach Brendon 'Baz' McCullum, wanted to make the team relax, enjoy their cricket, take risks and try out new things.

Ben was determined to lead from the front. Shortly after he was appointed captain, he played for Durham against Worcestershire in a County

Championship match. He smoked an incredible 161 runs from 88 balls and his score included an incredible 17 sixes. That's a century in sixes (well, actually, 102 runs – Ben also struck another 32 runs in fours).

With the captain setting the tone, England enjoyed an incredible summer.

They swept aside New Zealand, India and South Africa playing cavalier cricket. Jonny Bairstow thumped huge runs – 589 of them in just five innings. Joe Root cracked a couple of centuries. The captain scored a sparkling hundred as well. The crowds loved it, the media couldn't quite believe it and many wondered if it was possible to play this exciting style of cricket away from England.

"No one is worried about getting out – it's part of batting. Releasing that fear of failure is why we are getting results."
– Ben Stokes

In November 2022, England flew out to Pakistan, their first tour there for 17 years. The pitches in Pakistan can be flat and slow, so getting wickets can sometimes be a problem for touring teams. So can scoring runs quick enough to build up big enough scores to win the game. Slow and steady, without taking any risks, was the advice from the old pros.

Ben and Baz said: "No way!"

On the first day of the first Test at Rawalpindi in Pakistan, England went in to bat. A Test match day normally consists of 90 overs and teams may score 200, 250 or a little over 300 runs, if they're going well. Well, England's first day lasted only 75 overs because of bad light but it didn't matter as they scored: **506 runs!**

They ended the day on 506 for 4!

Four players, Zak Crawley, Ben Duckett, Ollie Pope and Harry Brook (in only his second Test match) all scored centuries in a single day. England rattled along at almost seven runs an over.

No one had seen anything like it.

This adventurous approach continued throughout the entire series. Ben set funky fields, putting fielders in all sorts of unusual positions and started innings with spinners like Jack Leach and Joe Root rather than his fast bowlers. The batters attacked throughout the series. Harry Brook averaged 93.6 runs every time he batted whilst, at one point, Joe Root batted left-handed instead of right!

England have only ever won two Test matches in Pakistan since their first visit in 1961. In a single month in 2022, they won three! They returned home as the first Test team of any nation to win a clean sweep of Test matches in Pakistan – what an achievement!

DID YOU KNOW?

Ben Stokes donated all his match fees from the 2022 Pakistan-England series to the Pakistan flood appeal as floods had devastated parts of the country earlier that year.

TIME!

Our whirlwind tour of cricket's most exciting, inspiring, and hilarious stories is at an end – but our book is not!

Turn the page to find a simple player's guide, a glossary plus quizzes to test your knowledge . . .

How to Play: Basics

The stories in this book cover just some of the extraordinary matches, feats and players from centuries of this incredible sport. But new records are being set all the time, and amazing new players are emerging.

Could you be one of them?

You may be playing cricket already, but if you're new to the game, we want to reassure you that the basic rules really *aren't* that complicated . . .

The basics

Cricket teams are made up of 11 players. One team bats while the other team bowls and fields. A competitive game always starts with a coin toss between the two captains – the winner gets to choose whether to bat or bowl first.

The captain of the fielding team also has the responsibility of picking the bowler and wicketkeeper, and deciding where the other nine players will stand. There are more than 35 different fielding positions to choose from!

The captain of the batting team decides which order their team are going to bat in Players bat in pairs, one at each end of the pitch. Their aim is to hit the ball and score as many runs as possible.

Scoring runs

There are several ways to score runs. A batter may hit a 'six', sending the ball over the boundary rope without touching the ground. They might hit a 'four', where the ball goes over the boundary rope but hits the ground on the way. Batters don't need to do any actual running when a six or a four is hit!

Getting out

While the aim of the batting team is to score as many runs as possible, the aim of the bowling team is to stop them – by getting their batters 'out'. There are lots of ways a batter can be out, but just five that commonly occur . . .

1. If a batter hits a ball and it doesn't go as far as the boundary, then the players must run between the two wickets, trying to reach the stumps before the fielders have time to collect the ball and throw it at the stumps. If the ball reaches the stumps first, this is called a 'run out'.

2. When the batter doesn't hit the ball but it hits the stumps instead they are 'out, bowled'!

3. When the batter hits the ball and it's caught by a fielder, they are 'out, caught'!

4. When a wicketkeeper gathers the ball and manages to hit the stumps whilst the batter is out of their crease, this is a 'stumping'.

5. When the batter doesn't hit the ball and it hits part of their body instead, they are out 'LBW' (leg before wicket).

Once a batter is out, they are replaced by the next player in the batting order. When ten of the 11 batters are out — or they reach the end of their overs (the number of overs depends on the format that's being played) – their 'innings' is over and the teams switch batting and bowling roles.

Matches are either one innings per side (like T20 matches) or two innings per side (like Test matches and first-class matches). The winner is the team with the most runs.

DID YOU KNOW?

The bowler may shout "Howzat!" to the umpire when the ball hits the batter's body. It's only LBW if the ball was heading towards the stumps. It can be a difficult decision for the umpire to make – it all happens so quickly!

Glossary

ASHES A long-running Test cricket series between England and Australia.

BAILS Two small pieces of wood that form part of the wicket, resting on the top of the three vertical stumps.

BATTER The player who stands opposite the bowler on the pitch and hits the ball with a bat after it has been bowled. Plays on the opposite team to the bowler and fielders.

BOUNDARY The line that runs around the edge of a cricket ground.

BOWLER The player who bowls the ball towards the batter. They usually take a run-up before they release to build some momentum and help them propel the ball forward faster. Plays on the same team as the fielders and the opposite team to the batter.

CAPTAIN Each team has a captain who makes decisions such as who should bowl and where the fielders should stand.

CENTURY When a batter scores 100 runs in a single innings. A half-century is 50 runs.

CREASE Horizontal lines going across the cricket pitch to determine where batters and bowlers are allowed to stand and move.

DUCK When a batter is dismissed without scoring any runs.

FAST BOWLER A bowler who bowls the ball at very quick speeds, sometimes over 140km per hour.

FIELD The grassy part of a cricket ground outside of the rectangular pitch.

FIELDER A player who stands in the field waiting to retrieve the ball after the batter has hit it – ideally by catching it, to get them out! They are on the same team as the bowler.

FOUR The score gained when a batter hits the ball and it bounces or rolls over the boundary without being picked up by a fielder.

INNINGS The part of a cricket match where one team is batting. An innings can end either when all the batters apart from one are out, or when there are a set number of overs which have been completed.

LBW (LEG BEFORE WICKET) One of the ways in which a batter can become 'out'. LBW happens when a ball would have hit the wicket, but instead hits part of the batter's body.

MID-OFF One of the many fielding positions on a cricket ground. This position is near to the bowler. There is also 'silly mid-off', which is even nearer to the batter.

NO-BALL This most often occurs when the bowler's front foot oversteps the popping crease as they're about to bowl. One run is added to the batting team's total and the ball has to be bowled again.

ODI (ONE DAY INTERNATIONAL) A style of cricket where a set number of overs is played. At the moment, One Day Internationals have 50 overs, typically lasting between seven and a half hours and a maximum of nine hours.

OUT When a batter is forced to finish their turn batting. This can happen in multiple ways, such as a fielder catching the ball, LBW, or the batter being stumped by the wicketkeeper.

OVER A set of six deliveries from the bowler to the batter (not including any illegal deliveries such as wide balls or no-balls).

PITCH The rectangular area of a cricket ground where the batters and wicket can be found during a match. Confusingly, the whole cricket ground is sometimes also called a pitch!

POPPING CREASE A line that runs horizontally across the cricket pitch, 122cm (4 feet) away from the stumps. The bowler has to keep part of their foot behind this line when they bowl, otherwise it will be a 'no-ball'.

RUNS The cricket scoring system, named because one 'run' is gained when a batter has travelled from one end of the pitch to the other.

SIX The number of runs gained when a batter hits the ball over the boundary without it touching the ground.

SPIN BOWLER A bowler who twists the ball at the moment they bowl it, causing it to change direction.

STUMP The upright part of a wicket.

STUMPING When a wicketkeeper gets a batter out by knocking the bails off the wicket while the batter is out of their ground.

T20 (TWENTY20) A short form of the game where each team plays just one innings, lasting up to 20 overs. It usually lasts two and a half to three hours.

TEST A type of cricket match that lasts up to five days, with players playing three sessions each day of about two hours each, with two breaks for lunch and tea in between.

UMPIRE A cricketing official, who stands on the pitch and makes decisions such as whether a batter is out, if a ball is wide, or if a bowler has bowled a no-ball.

WICKET A set of three vertical stumps with two horizontal bails balanced on top. There is one wicket at each end of the cricket pitch. Confusingly, the term 'wicket' is sometimes also used to refer to the pitch.

WICKETKEEPER A player who stands behind the wicket and tries to get the batter out by catching the ball or stumping them.

WIDE When a bowler bowls the ball too far to the right or left of the batter and wicket, or too high over their head.

Mix 'n' Match Super Stats

Can you match the player to the fact?
Find the answers on page 173.

B.S. Chandrasekhar

Anya Shrubsole

Brian Lara

Shafali Verma

Ben Stokes

Shane Warne

Ellyse Perry

Jimmy Anderson

MS Dhoni

Mignon du Preez

Betty Snowball

1. In 2005, this mighty bowler took a staggering 96 Test wickets in a year, at an average of 22 runs per wicket. It's the most taken by any Test bowler ever!

2. This iconic cricketer had ten brothers and sisters. In 2017, a new 15,000-seat stadium in Trinidad and Tobago was named after him.

3. This pioneering cricketer's skill with the bat is shown by an average of 40.86 runs every time they played an innings for England.

4. In 2021, this dazzling all-rounder became the first Australian cricketer, male or female, to achieve 5,000 runs and 300 wickets whilst playing for their country.

5. This demon Test bowler was not very good with the bat! He scored fewer Test match runs (167) than he took Test wickets (242).

6. Which talented female cricketer scored 5,684 runs for South Africa in all formats and took a single international wicket, in a 2018 ODI versus Bangladesh?

7. This powerhouse bowler has taken 507 wickets for England in international matches – and once took 5 for 11 against New Zealand in a T20 international.

8. Which superstar player holds the world record for the biggest innings (258 runs) made when batting six in a Test match?

9. This bowling genius managed to get legendary Indian batter Sachin Tendulkar out more often than any other fast bowler in the world (nine times in 14 Tests).

10. After the 2020 T20 World Cup, this rising star worked on her batting with the Ranji men's team. She would face 150 bouncers in a row to perfect her technique.

11 This record-breaking cricketer captained their country on 332 occasions – no player has been skipper more often. They also have the most stumpings of any wicketkeeper (195 in total).

Test Your Knowledge

Find the answers on page 173.

1. Who is India's most successful captain, winning 40 Tests between 2014 and 2022?

2. Who holds the record for the highest number of runs scored during the Ashes?

3. Which female cricketer also played international football, scoring at the FIFA Women's World Cup quarter-final in 2011?

4. What's the name given to a score of 111?

5. Who holds the record for the highest ever score in any first-class match . . . and what was the score?

6. Alongside Jack Hayward, who jointly founded the first Cricket World Cup?

7. What have you suffered if you are out without scoring or facing a ball?

8. Who scored the most Test runs in a single day . . . and what was the score?

9. What age was Sajjida Shah when she debuted for Pakistan in 2000?

10. What was the name of the match played at the top of Kilimanjaro, Tanzania?

11. Which year saw the launch of the Blind Cricket World Cup?

12. What is a 'dead ball'?

13. How long was the longest ever Test match, including rest days?

14. Who holds the record for the highest ever women's ODI score . . . and what is that score?

15. Which world record was set by Mahela Jayawardene and Kumar Sangakkara playing for Sri Lanka in 2006?

16. Who bowled the fastest known ball in cricket history?

17. Who donated their match fees from the 2022 Pakistan-England series to charity?

18. Who became England cricket's youngest male Test player in 2022?

19. Which legendary West Indies batter became the first player in history to score a century and take five wickets in an ODI match.

20. What's the name given to a ball bowled to land near the feet of the batter, making it hard to hit?

Mix 'n' Match Super Stats answers: 1. Shane Warne (page 104); **2.** Brian Lara (page 36); **3.** Betty Snowball (page 112); **4.** Ellyse Perry (page 18); **5.** B.S. Chandrasekhar (page 94); **6.** Mignon du Preez (page 122); **7.** Anya Shrubsole (page 46); **8.** Ben Stokes (page 152); **9.** James Anderson (page 26); **10.** Shafali Verma (page 84); **11.** MS Dhoni (page 131)

Test Your Knowledge answers: 1. Virat Kohli (page 138); **2.** Don Bradman (page 16); **3.** Ellyse Perry (page 18); **4.** Nelson (page 30); **5.** Brian Lara, 501 not out (page 36); **6.** Rachael Heyhoe Flint (page 56); **7.** A diamond duck (page 62); **8.** Don Bradman, 309 (page 67); **9.** 12 years old (page 70); **10.** Mr Kill Madness (page 73); **11.** 1998 (page 79); **12.** A ball that a batter can't score a run off (page 85); **13.** 12 days (page 98); **14.** Amelia Kerr, 232 (page 119); **15.** The highest partnership for any wicket in a Test match (page 140); **16.** Shoaib Akhtar (page 145); **17.** Ben Stokes (page 152); **18.** Rehan Ahmed (page 126); **19.** Sir Vivian Richards (page 92); **20.** A yorker (page 12)

Look out for more fun-filled books from Farshore!

Amazing Facts

Amazing Puzzles & Quizzes

Amazing Football Facts

AMAZING FACTS
EVERY 8 YEAR OLD NEEDS TO KNOW

AMAZING FACTS
EVERY 9 YEAR OLD NEEDS TO KNOW

AMAZING FACTS
EVERY 10 YEAR OLD NEEDS TO KNOW

AMAZING PUZZLES & QUIZZES
FOR EVERY 8 YEAR OLD

AMAZING PUZZLES & QUIZZES
FOR EVERY 9 YEAR OLD

AMAZING PUZZLES & QUIZZES
FOR EVERY 10 YEAR OLD

AMAZING FOOTBALL FACTS
EVERY 8 YEAR OLD NEEDS TO KNOW

AMAZING FOOTBALL FACTS
EVERY 9 YEAR OLD NEEDS TO KNOW

AMAZING FOOTBALL FACTS
EVERY 10 YEAR OLD NEEDS TO KNOW

CLIVE GIFFORD is an award-winning author of more than 200 books, including the official guide to the ICC Cricket World Cup 2019. His books have won the Blue Peter Children's Book Award, the Royal Society Young People's Book Prize, the School Library Association's Information Book Award and Smithsonian Museum's Notable Books For Children. Clive lives in Manchester within a short walk of Lancashire's Old Trafford cricket ground.

LU ANDRADE is an illustrator from Ecuador, currently living in the mountains of Quito. She has studied everything from cinematography to graphic design. After focusing on digital animation for four years, she turned her hand to illustration, working on projects including *Good Night Stories for Rebel Girls*.